CLOTHES & CRAFTS IN

ANCIENT EGYPT

Richard Balkwill

A ZOË BOOK

A ZOË BOOK

© 1998 Zoë Books Limited

Devised and produced by
Zoë Books Limited
15 Worthy Lane
Winchester
Hampshire SO23 7AB
England

First published in Great Britain in 1998 by
Zoë Books Limited
15 Worthy Lane
Winchester
Hampshire SO23 7AB

A record of the CIP data is available from the British Library.

ISBN 1 86173 005 5

Printed in Belgium by Proost N.V.
Editor: Kath Davies
Design & Production: Sterling Associates
Illustrations: Virginia Gray

Photographic acknowledgments

The publishers wish to acknowledge, with thanks, the following photographic sources:

C.M.Dixon 5b, 9b, 14tl & r, 22b / The Egyptian Museum, Cairo - title page, 5c, 10b, 13r, 23b / The British Museum, London 3, 4b, 6t & bl, 7t & b, 9t, 11t, 12b, 13l, 14b, 16b, 17t & b, 19t & b, 20, 21tl, 22t, 23t, 25t & b / The Louvre Museum, Paris 5t, 6br, 8tr, 11b, 12t, 16t, 21b, 24b / The National Archaeological Museum, Florence 8l & br, 15b, 18t / Deutsches Museum, Munich 10t / The Egyptian Museum, Berlin 15t, 18b, 24t / Musée Borely, Marseille 21 tr.

Cover: C.M.Dixon / The Egyptian Museum, Cairo, top left and centre / The Louvre Museum, Paris, top right, bottom left and right.

The publishers have made every effort to trace the copyright holders, but if they have inadvertently overlooked any, they will be pleased to make the necessary arrangement at the first opportunity.

CONTENTS

INTRODUCTION

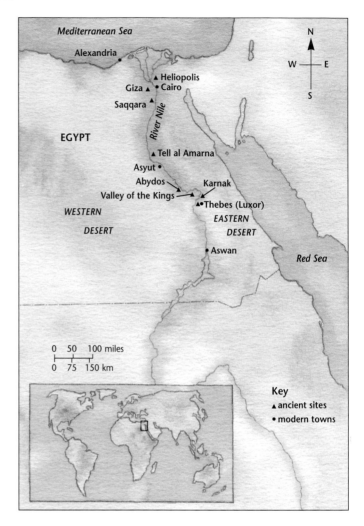

More than 5000 years ago, the people of Ancient Egypt lived in the valley of the River Nile, in North Africa. Every year, the river flooded, making the soil beside it fertile. Crops grew well in this soil, and there was always plenty to eat and drink.

The Egyptians were skilled in **crafts** such as pottery, painting and carving. They knew how to weave cloth for fine clothes, and how to make precious stones into jewellery. The Egyptians built magnificent palaces and elaborate tombs for their rulers, the Pharaohs. Painters decorated the walls of these buildings with scenes of everyday life, and pictures of gods and goddesses.

▶ Most of the land in Egypt is desert. You can see from the ancient sites and modern towns, that people lived by the River Nile.

For more than 2000 years Egypt was ruled by kings and queens. Historians of Egypt, called Egyptologists, divided this time into three main periods.

2500 - 2000 BC	Old Kingdom
2000 - 1500 BC	Middle Kingdom
1500 - 332 BC	New Kingdom

◀ This drawing comes from a papyrus book, made around 1250 BC. It shows a husband and wife wearing very fine clothes. They are standing in front of a table laden with offerings for the dead.

How do we know about the Egyptians?

People who study the things which other people made or built long ago are called **archaeologists**. They have found Egyptian paintings, carvings, writings and many other objects.

Rich Egyptians lived in homes with carved wooden furniture and beautiful decorations made of clay, glass and metals. They dressed in cool linen tunics, and kept themselves clean and sweet-smelling. Men and women wore jewellery, for decoration and to protect themselves from evil. Poor people wore little clothing as they worked under the hot sun.

There were not many trees in Egypt, but reeds called **papyrus** grew beside the River Nile. People made ropes, mats and even boats from papyrus, and a type of paper like **parchment**. Writers or scribes wrote on papyrus paper, and they have left us a full picture of life in Ancient Egypt.

▲ A bronze figure of Imhotep, the architect of the pyramid of Saqqara.

▼ Seti I ruled Egypt from 1318-1304 BC. The inside of his temple is covered with carvings.

▼ The gold mask on the coffin of the King Tutankamun, who died about 1327 BC. At this time, rulers were not buried in pyramids, but in tombs in the Valley of the Kings.

Things for the afterlife

The Egyptians believed that when people died, they went on a journey to the next life. They were buried with clothes, jewels, cooking pots and food for the journey. The walls of rich people's tombs, the **pyramids**, were covered with paintings. The dry climate has **preserved** many of these items, so we know what people wore and what they made.

ANCIENT EGYPTIAN CRAFTS

Papyrus

In the marshes beside the River Nile, thick beds of papyrus reed grew everywhere. Workers waded into the mud and shallow water to pull up the reeds. They tied up the reeds into bundles and brought them to workshops. Here workers would plait and twist the reed to make ropes, sandals, matting and boats.

Strips and layers of papyrus were soaked, pressed and then dried. These strips were joined together with gum and made into rolls of paper. Papyrus rolls, or scrolls, were kept in boxes and jars so that the ink did not fade. Sometimes the writing was washed off, and the rolls were used again!

▲ A papyrus painting of a man and wife playing **senet**, a popular board game.

How scribes worked

Scribes sat cross-legged with the papyrus roll resting on their knees. The writing material was stiff, so they did not need a flat surface such as a table to rest on.

▼ A man hunts in the papyrus beds beside the River Nile.

▼ This stone figure, found at Saqqara, is of a seated scribe.

Wood

Trees did not grow easily in the heat of the Egyptian desert. Sycamore and tamarisk trees grew beside the Nile, and palm and fig trees were plentiful. Wood for boats and coffins came from other countries.

Most houses in Egypt had little furniture, but there were wooden low tables, beds and even a kind of pillow to prop up people's heads. A carpenter used an axe and an **adze** to cut and shape wood. The blades of these tools were first made of flint. Later bronze and other hard metals were used.

Long planks of wood were very difficult to make. So joiners fastened small sections of wood together, one on top of the other, like tiles on a roof. Sometimes pieces were joined together by wooden pegs. This was skilfully done to make the sections of wood look like one piece.

► This mummy case was made in about 900 BC. It was found at Thebes.

◄ This wooden box belonged to a woman musician. It was made in 1000 BC.

The work of the woodcarver

Hard woods, such as ebony, were often **inlaid** with ivory. Carved wood was used to make **mummy** cases. The wood was hollowed out into the shape of the wrapped body, or mummy, which it would contain. Adults, children and even cats and dogs were buried in these cases.

▶ A detail from a beautifully decorated glazed tile, shows cattle grazing in the marshes.

Pottery

Potters used clay to make household objects such as storage jars for wine or water, bowls, flasks for oil and huge pots for storing grain. Clay dolls and toys have been found, too.

There was plenty of clay in Egypt. The first potters took the clay or **silt** from places near the banks of the River Nile. They sometimes mixed it with sand to make it easier to work. The potters shaped the clay by **moulding** it, or by building it up in thin coils. They smoothed the outside and decorated it with simple **geometric** patterns, or painted it red or black. The clay was baked hard in the hot sun.

▲ This storage jar has been decorated with geometric patterns, using blue, red and black paints.

▲ You can see vase-painters at work, on this carved relief from an Egyptian tomb. It was made around 1372-1354 BC.

Later, during the Middle Kingdom, people invented the types of potters' wheel and firing **kiln** that are still used today.

Bricks

The floodwaters of the River Nile left behind mud and silt. The bricks which were used to build houses and some of the pyramids and tombs were made of these materials.

Brickmakers mixed straw or sand with the mud and clay.

▼ Millions of bricks were used to help build this pyramid at Giza in about 2500 BC. Brick and earth ramps were made so that the huge stone blocks could be put into position more easily. The carved head of the sphinx is on the right.

They put the mixture into wooden moulds, and left it to dry in the hot sun. An outside coating of limestone was sometimes added to make the bricks stronger. Bricks were often decorated with a stamp to show the name or symbol of the pharaoh for whom they had been made.

◄ The lid of this pottery storage jar represents a god, Duamutef, who had the head of a jackal.

A bed of bricks

Mud bricks were used to make a bench outside houses. Young workers or guards could sleep on the bench as the nights were always dry.

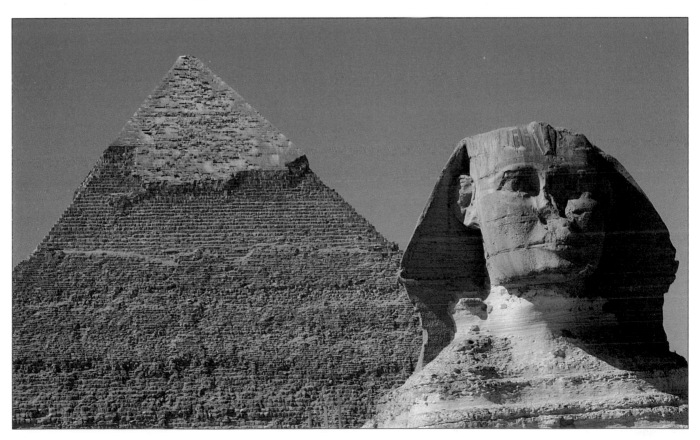

Glass

Pliny was a Roman historian who lived many hundreds of years after the time of the Ancient Egyptians. He wrote that some Egyptian merchants invented glass by accident. They lit a fire on a sandy beach. They rested their cooking pots on lumps of natron (a kind of soda). In the morning, they noticed that some natron and sand had melted and made a shiny, hard material – glass.

Historians now say that this story is not quite correct. However, it is true that from the time of the Middle Kingdom onwards, the Egyptians knew how to make glass.

▲ A glass jar made between 1500 and 200 BC, before glass blowing was used in Egypt.

Egyptian glass facts

- Glass was used to make small jars for perfume or ointment, and for jewellery.
- Glass blowing was not known in Egypt until Roman times.
- Modern glass is heated to temperatures of 1500°Celsius. Furnaces in Egypt could only reach 1000°C, so the glass had little bubbles of air in it.

Glassmakers heated sand and mixed it with lime and plant ash. They did not blow glass into shape. First they

▶ This pendant was found in the tomb of Tutankamun. It depicts the vulture of Upper Egypt. The pendant is made of gold and decorated with **enamel**.

◀ You can see where the bright blue glaze, or *faience*, has worn off this figurine which was made around 600 BC. The sow and her piglets were sacred to the Egyptian sky-goddess, Nut.

moulded a mixture of clay and weeds or leaves on to a stick, and shaped it like the inside of a jar. They dipped this into molten glass, and wrapped coils of soft glass round it. They used copper and **cobalt** to colour the glass green or blue. The outside of the glass was smoothed and decorated. Then the glass was baked in a furnace.

▲ A *faience* amulet of Bes, a god who protected people from evil.

After the glass had cooled, the mixture inside it was broken up and removed through the neck of the jar.

Faience

Egyptian craftworkers made objects to look like precious stones. The objects were made from a thick paste of sand mixed with ash or lime with a bright blue glaze on the outside. This material is now called ***faience***.

The oldest Egyptian *faience* objects were beads and necklaces. Later, there were statues of animals, beautiful bowls and jars. Some were decorated with birds and lotus leaves.

Lucky charms

- Tiny lucky charms are called **amulets**.
- The word amulet comes from the Arabic word meaning 'protection from evil'.
- Egyptian men and women wore amulets around their necks to keep them safe.

Metals

The most common metals found in Ancient Egypt were copper, tin and iron. Metalworkers, or smelters, also made bronze (a mixture of copper and tin). Hard metals were used to make sharp blades for tools or weapons. Softer metals, like lead, were used to make containers for water, or to cover wood or stone to make it last longer.

▲ These gold and **lapis-lazuli** figures of the Egyptian gods, Osiris, Horus and Isis were made between 950 and 730 BC.

Huge bronze statues and carvings have been found in tombs, but Egyptians also made smaller articles like cups, bowls and jewellery out of copper and bronze.

A god with iron bones

Iron was not widely used in Egypt. Even in the dry climate, a red rust would form on the metal. Egyptians believed that this colour showed the work of Set, the god of evil, whose bones were said to be made of iron.

◀ This bronze figure of a falcon, which was painted and inlaid with gold, was made around 590 BC. He carries a solar disc and wears a neck decoration of the Egyptian sun god, Ra.

Gold and silver

Gold was very highly valued by the Egyptians. Its yellow colour, like that of the sun, was thought to be the work of the gods. The wealthiest people wore gold jewellery. The finest and richest of treasures found in the tombs of the Pharaohs were made in solid gold, such as the famous portrait mask which covered Tutankamun's head. It weighs over 10 kilogrammes.

A Greek historian called Diodorus describes a gold mining town in the south of Egypt. Hundreds of workers lived in stone huts, each with a granite hand mill. They used the mills to crush **quartz**. The quartz dust was then washed and tiny flecks of gold collected for **smelting**. Work went on day and night. Workers were chained and beaten, and not allowed to

▲ The gold mask on the mummy case of Tutankamun.

stop work even when they became ill. Over it all, the sun burned down on this harsh desert place.

Silver, a softer metal, was not found in Egypt. It was imported and used to make jewellery. It was also mixed with gold to make electron. This mixture was whiter or paler than gold in colour, and used to make ornamental vases.

▲ A silver statue, decorated with gold foil, which was made around 900 BC.

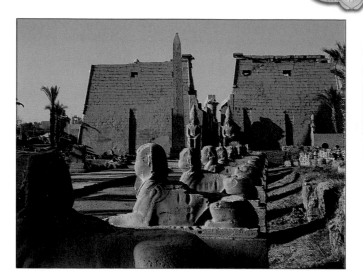

▲ The temple to Amun, one of the most important Egyptian gods, was built at Luxor by the ruler Amenhotep III. Work started around 1350 BC and finished around 1213 BC. The avenue leading from the temple is lined by stone-carved sphinxes. The avenue was used for processions between Karnak and Luxor.

Stone

In Ancient Egypt, before the Old Kingdom, people carved stone to make their tools and weapons. Flint was used for the tips of arrows, and for the blades of knives and daggers.

◀ A sandstone sculpture of an Egyptian high priest, made around 1900 BC.

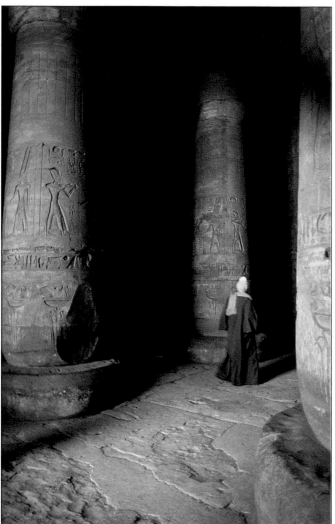

▲ Huge carved pillars in the hall of the temple of Seti I, at Abydos, which was built around 1300 BC.

Many of the pyramids in Ancient Egypt are made from soft limestone, which was found everywhere. Harder stone, such as white limestone, granite and **alabaster** were dug out of special quarries.

Stonemasons made huge statues and **obelisks** from granite and alabaster. There are many famous paintings of these huge carvings. The paintings show how the figures were moved, either by boat or on rollers. One picture shows an alabaster statue 13 cubits (about 6 metres) high, of a prince called Dhuthotep. 172 men are

◄ A stone relief of a horse's head made around 1300 BC. It was found at Tell al Armana.

Pictures in stone

Many scenes of Ancient Egypt were carved directly into the stone on the inside walls of tombs. The lines of the picture were cut in the rock or stone, leaving the image standing out in relief.

▼ A painted relief of Maat, the Egyptian goddess of truth, made around 1300 BC.

dragging the statue, harnessed by four long ropes, while overseers shout commands.

Precious stones

Egyptian men and women wore jewellery for decoration, as well as *amulets* to keep them safe. People wore collars and necklaces of gold, glass and precious stones. Jewels such as amethyst, cornelian and lapis lazuli were inlaid into metal frames, or carved and fitted into rings. Women wore anklets and bracelets, and sometimes a golden girdle around the waist. Earrings were also common.

Jewellery for the dead

Jewellery was placed on the dead to help them in their journey to the next life. Rich people had rings made of gold. Poor people had to make do with rings made of carved glass, or even straw. An ornament was placed over the heart, to protect it from evil spirits.

Painting

We know a great deal about life in Ancient Egypt thanks to the artists who painted on the inside walls of tombs. The darkness and the dry climate have preserved these pictures well.

Egyptian painters often showed a complete story in one picture. They painted people from the side, not from the front.

The artist's palette

Egyptian painters had few colours to choose from. Red and yellow came from the ochre found in iron and sulphur. Blue came from azurite, and green from **malachite**. Soot and **gypsum** were used to make black paint. Brushes for painting large areas were made from bundles of palm. For finer work, painters chewed the end of a piece of wood to make bristles.

Scribes

Writers, or scribes, were slaves. They were also very important because most people could not read or write. The job of writing

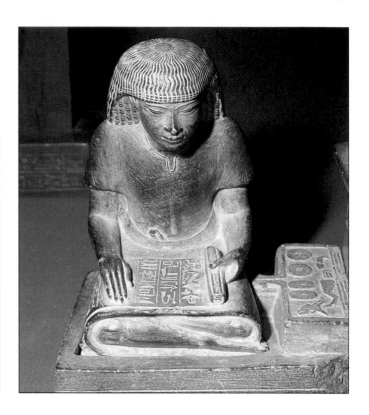

▲ A stone carving of the royal scribe and reader-in-chief, Nebmertouf

◀ A wall painting from a tomb at Thebes, made around 1400 BC. It shows a horse, chariot and an attendant.

Scribes did not write poetry or stories to entertain. They made a record of laws, agreements and levels of taxes, or of events in the homes of rich people.

Scribes used brushes and ink to write on papyrus. Papyrus reeds were used to make brushes. Ink was made by adding water to soot or **charcoal**, or to minerals which had been ground up.

▲ A papyrus painting made around 1340-1300 BC, by a scribe called Hakhte.

was often handed down from father to son. Girls were not taught to be scribes.

Ancient Egyptian writing is made of many tiny pictures, called **hieroglyphs**. The word comes from two Greek words meaning 'sacred carvings'. Pictures form each letter, and often look like the object they stand for.

Which way round?

Ancient Egyptian hieroglyphs can be written starting from the left, starting from the right, or starting at the top and going down. How do you know where to start reading? Just look at which way the animals and people are facing – they always face towards the beginning of the line.

Counting in Ancient Egypt

The Egyptian counting system was based on the number 10.
100 was shown by a coil of rope.
1000 was a lotus flower.
10000 showed a finger.
100000 was represented by a tadpole.

▲ A list of offerings for a state official, which shows the hieroglyph for 100 (a coil of rope) very clearly.

CLOTHES AND JEWELLERY

Grass, reeds and a tough plant called hemp were also used to make cloth, but this was most often turned into matting. Historians disagree about the use of wool.

The most common material used to make clothing in Egypt was linen. Linen is made from a plant called **flax**. The young, green plants were used to make fine thread. When the plant turned yellow, it was best for making linen cloth. When fully ripe, it was used to make mats and ropes. The finest material, worn by rich people, was called 'royal linen'.

▲ This limestone relief, made around 1372-1354 BC, shows shoe-makers at work.

Leather

Leather was widely used to make thick clothes, or shoes. Vellum was a fine leather which was used to write on.

◀ A wall painting from the 14th century BC shows a man and woman dancing. Both are wearing fine linen clothes, and decorated collars. You can see that the man is wearing sandals.

It seems likely that wool was used to make warm clothes, such as cloaks to wear in the desert when the nights were cold. Cotton and silk came into Egypt at the end of the New Kingdom, about 2300 years ago.

Weaving and dyeing

The flax stems, or **fibres**, were first dried and then rolled to form threads. This process was called roving. Spindles were then used to spin the thread which was wound into balls. The threads were then placed on a **loom** and woven to form cloth. Men did most of the weaving jobs. The main task of women was to train and supervise the workers in the workshops.

People have used plants to make dyes for cloth for thousands of years. Blue came from plants called woad and indigo. Madder and **henna** gave red colours. Yellow came from the saffron crocus, and could be mixed with indigo to make green.

▲ A detail from a papyrus painting which shows a man wearing white linen clothes.

◀ Ramses III, who ruled Egypt from about 1184-1153 BC, is on the right of the painting. He stands in front of three Egyptian gods. They all wear different styles of clothes and elaborate headdresses.

Clothes in life and death

The dry, dark conditions in ancient Egyptian tombs have helped to preserve some of the cloth inside, so we do know something about clothes and the materials used to make them.

Paintings and carvings can also provide clues to what people wore. But archaeologists have to be careful about drawing conclusions. People sometimes insisted that they were shown wearing their best clothes, or in clothes of an earlier time. People loved to look good, and remember old times, just as they do today!

Clothes for the dead

In the tombs of the wealthy, the bodies were sometimes dressed in their finest robes.

Other people were simply wrapped in strips of cloth, torn from old clothes. These words were said at the funeral of someone who lived in the New Kingdom: 'She who was rich in fine linen, who loved clothes, lies in the cast-off garments of yesterday.'

▼ This papyrus painting shows a ceremony which took place just before the mummy was placed in the tomb. You can see strips of cloth on the mummy, which is held by Anubis, the Egyptian god of the dead.

▲ A woman from the Old Kingdom wears a tube dress.

▲ A man from the New Kingdom wears pleated clothes.

Simple clothes for the heat

In the oldest times, women wore a simple tube dress. A piece of linen was sewn down one side, and straps added at the top held the dress over the shoulders. White was a symbol of purity, so the material was often left undyed. Later, collars with coloured patterns were added. In the New Kingdom, there was much more decoration and bright colour in clothes.

Men in the Old Kingdom wore a simple kilt. They wrapped a piece of cloth round the middle of the body, and fastened it at the waist.

By the time of the Middle Kingdom, the kilt had become longer and straighter, while fringes and pleats were added later, in the time of the New Kingdom. In Ancient Egypt, no-one wore underwear.

◀ This wooden figure shows a man wearing a simple kilt.

Pleats

Pleats, or folds, were made by pressing the fabric on to a wooden board with grooves in it. The pleats were kept in place by a type of starch.

Clothes for different occasions

Most children wore a simple **loin cloth** or tunic dress. But in the palaces of the rich, children wore the same elegant uniforms and dresses as their parents.

Dress gave an idea of rank. A lord might wear a broad band of cloth over his cloak to show his authority. The overseer of workers might wear a narrow band or ribbon around his neck to show his position.

Egyptians loved to dress up for a special occasion. Rich people wore beautiful clothes. Women and men wore long skirts or dresses fastened by clasps or brooches of precious metal. Sometimes they wore the patterned skin of an animal, such as a panther, over the shoulders.

▶ A wall painting from Thebes, made in the 12th century BC, showing the Pharaoh Amenhotep I.

Royal dress

Kings were often dressed as warriors. Queens sometimes wore long transparent dresses made from a very fine linen.

◀ This detail from a wall painting at Luxor shows a pharaoh and his son dressed for a special occasion.

Washing and mending clothes

Egyptians took pride in keeping their clothes clean. The jobs of Royal Chief Washer or Royal Chief Bleacher were very important. These jobs were done by men.

They washed the linen clothes on the banks of the River Nile. Many clothes were stained by the coloured wax which people placed on their heads at feasts, and which melted into their clothes. Dirty linen was rolled up into a ball, soaked in water and then rubbed with a soap called natron. Clean linen was folded and locked in boxes.

Laundry clues

Scribes copied out laundry lists, and some of these lists have survived. From them we can tell the kinds of clothes that rich people wore.

▼ An Egyptian sculpture of the wife of a prince was made around 2600-2500 BC. The embroidered headband keeps her wig in place.

▲ Queen Ahmose Nefertari (1575-1505 BC) may have outlived her son, Amenhotep I.

Sewing and mending

Needles and thimbles have survived. They were used for embroidering cloth, sewing decorations on clothes, and for mending.

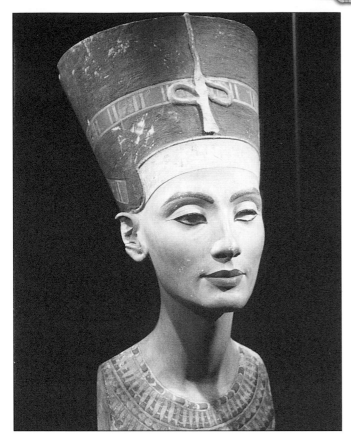

▲ Queen Nefertiti, who ruled Egypt when her husband died in 1335 BC. The front of her crown carries the symbol of a rearing cobra, or *uraeus*, which was thought to protect the ruler.

Headdresses

- Some people wore headdresses to show their position or rank. Some were embroidered or decorated with gold or jewels.
- The pharaoh wore a crown on special occasions. At other times he wore a royal headcloth.
- Sometimes the pharaoh wore a red and white crown. White was the colour for Upper Egypt and red was the colour for Lower Egypt.

▼ A lady wearing a wig held in place by a gold headband.

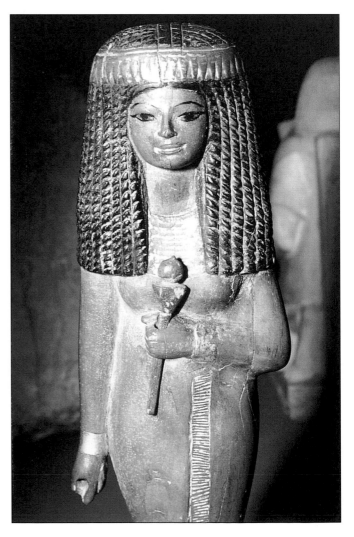

Shoes

In the Old and Middle Kingdom, most Egyptians walked barefoot. In later times, men wore sandals made of papyrus or leather. They were forbidden to wear them inside houses, or in the presence of someone superior to them.

Make-up

Men and women used make-up or cosmetics to give colour and beauty to their appearance. A powder called *kohl* was used to darken the skin around the eyes. Rouge was used on the cheeks and lips. People used mirrors made of polished copper or bronze.

Hair and wigs

The Egyptians were very careful about keeping clean. Young children had their heads shaved bald. As they got older, children grew their hair. Rich boys and girls had their hair plaited by servants every day. Women wore their hair long.

On special occasions rich women also wore elaborate wigs with decorated headbands. Wigs were often made into long plaits or tresses. The wigs were often made of human hair, but sometimes sheep's wool was used. Poorer women sold their hair to the wig-makers.

Many men in Ancient Egypt also shaved their heads and wore wigs. They shaved their faces to keep cool and clean. No one had a moustache. A beard was a sign of authority or wisdom, and rulers wore a false beard at feasts or festivals. On these occasions, women wore lotus flowers in their hair. Both men and women wore ointments and perfumes.

▲ A seated man is wearing a wig and a false beard. The painting is on a coffin lid made around 1050 BC.

Scented wax

Guests at banquets sometimes placed a cake or ball of scented wax on their heads. During the heat of a long evening, the wax melted and gave off a sweet scent.

◀ These musicians are playing at a banquet. You can see the cones of wax on their heads.

FESTIVALS AND FUN

The Ancient Egyptians held festivals at different times of the year. Most festivals were held in honour of their many gods and goddesses. Ordinary people were given holidays so that they could take part in the processions and celebrations at the temple which was the 'home' of a particular god or goddess. Some texts from the Middle and New Kingdoms told people to enjoy themselves throughout their lives. One says: '... cease not to drink, to eat... Have holidays and do what you please every day and night.'

Getting ready for a feast

People in Ancient Egypt loved parties. They sometimes held feasts which lasted all day. They invited special guests, and everyone wore their best clothes. Men and women wore jewellery and make-up.

Imagine that you are going to an Egyptian feast. You will wear a jewelled collar, and paint your face so that you will look your best.

Paint your face like an Ancient Egyptian

You will need: • black and red face paints, or black eye-liner and red lipstick • a mirror.

1. Close one eye. Remember to keep it closed until the paint dries. Starting next to your nose, paint a thick, black line along your eye-lid, just above your eye-lashes. Continue the line about 1-2cm beyond your eye.

2. Paint another line above the first one.

3. Paint a thick black line along your eyebrow. Take it as far as the other lines. Let the paint dry.

4. Do the same for the other eye.

5. Use the paint or lipstick to colour your lips red.

Make a decorated collar

You will need: • a pencil • a ruler • some thick paper or card (about 40cm x 30cm) • a pair of scissors • paints or colouring pencils • 2 safety pins.

1. Place the paper with the long edges at the top and bottom. Fold it in half, from left to right.

2. Use your ruler to measure 12cm along the top left-hand edge. Mark the point with your pencil. Now mark 8cm down the left-hand side. Draw a curved line between these points. Draw a curved line from the top right-hand corner to the bottom left-hand corner. Cut along these curved lines.

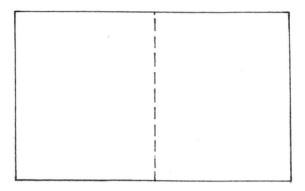

3. Open out the paper. Make four pencil marks along the top of each side of your collar, to divide it into five. Draw a curved line from one side to the other, between each pair of marks.

4. Decorate your collar using paints or pencils. You could copy the one in the picture, or use some of the other patterns for collars that you have seen earlier in this book.

5. When the collar is ready, pin it to your clothes at the shoulders with the two safety pins.

The snake game

Children in Ancient Egypt loved toys and games. Toy animals were very popular. There was a horse on wheels which children could pull or push along. Craftworkers usually made toys out of wood or clay.

The snake game was a bit like snakes and ladders. Children played it on a stone board or plate. The children used sticks that had one curved side and one flat side. They threw the sticks in the air, then counted how many landed with the flat side up. There were no dice in Ancient Egypt. Make a snakeboard and play this game.

You will need: • a piece of thick paper or card (about 20cm x 30cm) • a pencil • a black felt-tip pen • some colouring pens, paints or pencils • a pair of scissors • lollipop sticks.

1.   Draw a big snake on the paper, like the one in the picture. Draw four small circles – these will be your counters.

2.   Paint the snake yellow and the jewels on its neck red, blue and green. Paint each counter a different colour. When the paint is dry, use the black felt-tip pen to mark out the playing squares on the snake's body. Paint some of the squares red.

3.   Cut out the snake and the counters.

4.   Draw or paint a red snake on one side of each of the lollipop sticks. These will be your throwing sticks. Now you are ready to play your game.

5.   Up to four people can play, or you could play on your own by racing two counters against each other. Start each counter on the snake's head. Take turns to throw the six sticks in the air. When they land, count the number of sticks which show the snake. That is the number of squares you can move your counter along the snake. Beware! If you land on a red square, you must go back to the beginning. The winner is the first player who reaches the snake's tail.

Make an Egyptian pot

Egyptian craftworkers made pots and bowls from clay, stone and glass. People used pots at home and at work. The best pieces were kept for special occasions. You can make an Egyptian pot to hold your favourite things.

You will need • some clay (the sort that dries hard) • paints and a brush • a lollipop stick or a blunt knife.

1. Look at the pictures of pots, and choose which type of pot to make.

2. Break off lumps from your clay and roll the lumps into sausage shapes.

3. Coil a sausage around to make a base for your pot. Now coil more sausages to build up the shape of the pot. Make the clay stick by wetting it with a little water, or by pressing the joints together.

4. Use your stick or knife to smooth the surface of the pot. Let it dry.

5. When the clay is hard, you can paint it. Choose a reddish-orange, turquoise blue, black, white and yellow. Some Egyptian pots are all one colour, others have patterns like the ones in the picture.

GLOSSARY

adze:	A sharp cutting tool for shaping wood.
alabaster:	Stone used for carving figures.
amulet:	A decoration made of stone, wood or glass, worn to protect the wearer against evil.
archaeologist:	Someone who studies the past by digging up or examining ancient ruins, remains and writings.
charcoal:	Pieces of burned, blackened wood, used for drawing or for making ink.
cobalt:	A grey metal which is used to make blue colouring for pottery, glazes or glass.
craft:	Any trade or pastime in which people use skill to make things by hand.
enamel:	A glassy coating applied to metal or other surfaces and then fired or baked to harden it.
faience:	A thick paste made from sand or quartz mixed with lime, and coloured blue or green.
fibres:	Strong, thread-like parts of a plant.
flax:	A plant whose tough, stringy stems are used to make linen.
geometric:	Made up of repeated lines and angles, such as zig-zags.
gypsum:	A mineral of calcium and sulphur. Alabaster is a kind of gypsum.
henna:	A red dye, made from plants, used to colour hair.
hieroglyph:	The script used by Ancient Egyptians. It was made up of many tiny pictures or symbols. These symbols represent words and sounds.
inlaid:	Pieces of decorative material, such as stone or glass, set into a background. The background is carved so that the decoration fits exactly and the surfaces are level.
kiln:	An oven which can heat material such as clay to a very high temperature.
lapis-lazuli:	A blue semi-precious stone.
loin cloth:	A piece of cloth wrapped round the waist, sometimes hanging like a very short skirt, or passed between the legs, like a pair of shorts.
loom:	A wooden frame for weaving thread into cloth.
malachite:	A green mineral of copper that can be easily polished to a shine. Azurite is blue malachite.

moulding: Working something into a particular shape by hand, or pouring or pressing it into a hollow form, called a mould.

mummy: A dead body which was preserved with ointments. The body was wrapped tightly with strips of cloth.

obelisk: A tall, four-sided pillar, narrowing at the top.

papyrus: A reed which grows at the edge of the River Nile. The reeds were peeled and cut into strips. The strips were soaked in water to make them soft, then pressed and dried to form a sheet.

parchment: Paper made from papyrus or leather.

preserve: To stop from decaying, or going bad.

pyramids: The stone burial places of pharaohs and rich nobles. The four sloping sides stood on a square base. The sides met at a point at the top.

quartz: A mineral which has many different forms, including some gemstones. Quartz sometimes contains precious metals.

senet: A popular Egyptian board game which was played like draughts.

silt: The fine mud which is left behind by river floods. Egyptians used it for making bricks.

smelting: Heating metal to shape it into weapons, tools or decoration.

Further reading

Ancient Egypt, Judith Crosher, 'Technologies in the Time of' series (Wayland Publishers Limited, 1997)

Egyptians, R.Wright, 'Craft Topics' series (Watts Publishing Group, 1992)

The Egyptians and the Valley of the Kings, Philip Steele, 'Hidden Worlds' series (Zoë Books Limited, 1994)

Food & Feasts in Ancient Egypt, Richard Balkwill, 'Food and Feasts' series (Wayland Publishers Limited, 1994)

How Would you Survive as an Ancient Egyptian?, J.Morley, 'How Would you Survive?' series (Watts Publishing Group, 1993)

Over 3000 Years ago: In Ancient Egypt, Philip Sauvain, 'History Detective' series (Zoë Books Limited, 1993)

Pyramid, Rosalind Hall, 'Eyewitness Guides' (Shire Publications, 1986)

INDEX

PRINTED IN BELGIUM BY

INTERNATIONAL BOOK PRODUCTION